JESUS MAKES

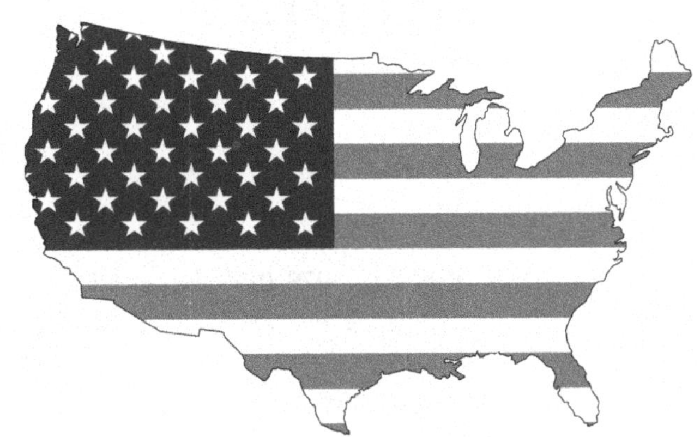

AMERICA GREAT™

ACTS ONE EIGHT
Publishing

JESUS
MAKES

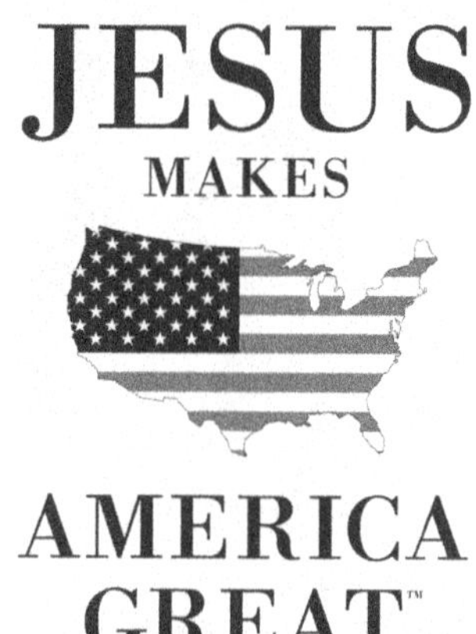

AMERICA GREAT™

STEVEN ANDREW

Paperback ISBN-13: 978-0-9986682-9-1
eBook: ISBN-13: 978-0-9986682-8-4

November 28, 2017.
Published by ACTS ONE EIGHT Publishing™
ActsOneEightPublishing.com

Scriptures are from the King James Version (KJV).

Contents

I am praying for you. Soon you will discover the safety, strength, and Biblical prosperity that come by following Jesus Christ. You will know God better, and He will be glorified in your life and in our Christian nation.

God has blessed me with exceptional people to review the manuscripts. I thank God for each person and I pray for God to strengthen each of you in Him.

Preface

The 9-11 Cross testifies of God's covenant through Jesus Christ with the USA. The 17 foot steel beam cross was found whole and then displayed.

"I am from above... I am not of this world." Jesus Christ

John 8:23 KJV

You are about to learn the truth of America that brings God's special protection, power, and abundance to you, your loved ones, and the nation.

The Bible says there is only one way to make America great. Our Christian founding fathers affirm this same truth. Will you join me in following Jesus Christ to make the USA exceptional again? I hope you will.

Steven Andrew
Pastor, USA Christian Church - www.USA.church
"Blessed is the nation whose God is the LORD"
Psalm 33:12 KJV

1
Who Makes America Great?

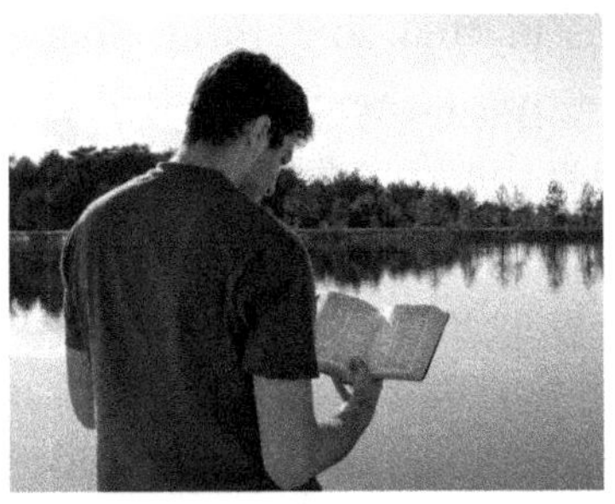

"I am the light of the world" Jesus Christ
John 8:12 KJV

Christ "In whom are hid all the treasures
of wisdom and knowledge."
Colossians 2:3 KJV

The key to having God's safety, strength, and prosperity for Americans is found by answering an important question: Who does God say makes America great? After all, His Word is what matters.

This book gives you the answer. Then it provides you with God's step-by-step plan to make the USA great. God's solution is the only way that brings you His protection, abundance, and freedom. Our founders followed this plan in 1776 to make our extraordinary nation. It always works!

Have you wondered, "What makes America exceptional? What is it that causes America to have God's favor, so that we are not a common country overridden with selfish people, corruption, and hurting individuals?"

Often, people think that safety and prosperity are the USA's significance. While it does mean this to some amount, the Bible informs us that something greater produced these blessings we enjoy. Others say democracy made them possible. However, the founders taught that democracies lead to mob rule, and the Constitution states the USA is a Christian Republic, wherein *we the people* are in charge.[1]

Some believe our nation's superiority means freedom to do anything, even if it is against God and America. But how do acts of treason—such as burning the American flag, or schools teaching young men that they might be women—make the USA great? The Declaration of Independence says our rights are from God, and George Washington said, "It is the duty of nations... to do His will".[2]

However, before we understand God's will and learn His answer, we must look at the reasons we need to be great again. This is urgent, because our lives, the country, and our national identity are at stake. Millions of people are in danger.

We Have Gone Astray from God's Word

We are in a national emergency situation. A Biblical analysis of the news shows that our lives are at risk because of our national sins. Opposing the LORD with false gods, homosexuality, and other sins does not make the USA great. Our forefathers remind us, "Righteousness exalts a nation, but sin is the reproach of any people" (Proverbs 14:34 KJV).

Our well-being is determined by our obedience to God's Word. God is in control. He gives us a Bible principle that He gives good leaders that care for us and protect liberty as His blessing, but bad politicians (the swamp) are a sign of God's judgment (Judges 2:11 - 4:2). Scripture says, *Be not deceived; God is not mocked,* and explains that sowing sin reaps corruption (Galatians 6:7-8 KJV). The good news is, because of the people doing the powerful *7 Bible Truths* in this book, God is ending judgments we have seen. Yet, some remain.

God showed the USA mercy with President Donald Trump, who says, "America first!" Barack Obama and Hillary Clinton were God's judgment. They persecuted Christians, falsely called Bible believers "haters" and "deplorables," and acted as swamp dictators. They colluded with Russia as traitors and sold 20% of our uranium to our enemies. Millions of people in the USA could die from a nuclear bomb because of this. The Bible says Hillary and Obama hate America and they were God's judgment for the nation disobeying the Holy Bible and doing covenant breaking acts: *...if ye shall despise my statutes, or if your soul abhor my judgments, so that ye will not do all my commandments, but that ye break my covenant: I also will do this unto you...* ***they that hate you shall reign over you;*** (Leviticus 26:14-17 KJV).

On the other hand, President Trump says he loves America, so we see God ended part of this judgment. Yet, when Congress, courts and the media oppose the President following God, we know God's judgment is not over.

As Christians, we thank God the president says, "In America we worship God, not government," is pro-life, quotes the Bible, and wants pastors to speak freely. Christians support President Trump where he follows Jesus Christ!

Some people think that politicians are in control, but God is the one who blesses or judges the nation. By the sovereignty of God, He directs leaders based on the nation's obedience to Him. *The king's heart is in the hand of the LORD, as the rivers of water: he turns it whithersoever he will* (Proverbs 21:1 KJV).

Others think we can be idle and sit back with President Trump, but the church not working to advance the Kingdom of our Lord Jesus Christ would mean more corruption. A strong church causes the USA to be great.

There is something we must remember. God is holy and our Judge. He cares for us and lets us know disobeying His Word causes troubles. It is one thing to unintentionally sin and then confess it to God and be forgiven. But to not repent or to publicly oppose Him by saying that sins, such as abortion, are "civil rights" provokes God, and judgment follows. *When the land sinneth against me... then will I stretch out mine hand upon it* (Ezekiel 14:13 KJV).

The Greatest Danger to Our Safety and Prosperity

God gives different judgments for different sins. False gods and sodomite societies result in the strongest judgments of invasion, captivity, and destruction. History records that all of these judgments happened to Israel. For this reason, it is urgent to understand that the nation's biggest danger is sin.

Those who forget God and *walk after other gods... shall surely perish* (Deuteronomy 8:19 KJV). Tolerance of false gods is a common sin and it rightfully angers a holy God. Muslims deny that God has a Son. The Bible says that such a denial is "antichrist" (1 John 2:22 KJV). Yet, Obama, Clinton, and the Democrat Party prayed often with Muslims, joining with them in worshipping a god who opposes Jesus Christ and Christians. There are major differences between Christianity and Islam. For example, Jesus Christ teaches to "love your enemies," but to be "wise" to prevent them from harming you. However, the Koran teaches to kill Christians, Jews, and others. That is why Muslims have a history of violence.

It is not just Democrats, but Republicans pray with other gods. There were Muslim and Sikh prayers at the 2016 GOP National Convention[3] and the National Cathedral included Hindu, Mormon, Islamic, and other non-Christian speakers after Trump's inauguration.[3] The Bible says interfaith prayer causes God's wrath, as when people served Baal and Molech.

Some say it is tolerance to accept those with other gods, but God's Word reveals this sin has put our lives and nation in danger of God's judgment of war. There is a common misconception that other religions, such as Mormonism, are good. We see most pastors are silent that the GOP chair is a Mormon cult member (Mitt Romney's niece). Mormons believe the evil lies that God was first a man and Jesus is the spirit brother of Lucifer. How can blaspheming God be good?

God says, Sodom and Gomorrah *giving themselves over to fornication, and going after strange flesh, are set forth for an example, suffering the vengeance of eternal fire* (Jude 7 KJV). God's judgment for same-sex marriage could be brimstone and fire, a nuclear war, or other destruction (Genesis 19:24).

Yet, Obama, the Clintons, the Supreme Court, schools, the military, businesses, and others have provoked God with homosexual and transgender sin, which God says is "abomination" (Leviticus 18:22, Deuteronomy 22:5). For example, the Air Force relieved a Senior Master Sergeant of duty for refusing to support the beliefs of a lesbian commander.[4]

Safety is God's blessing. Yet, one of the judgments that has not ended is terrorism. The Bible says false gods, same-sex marriage, and other sins are what cause terrorism. The judgment of terror is a curse from disregarding God's Word and covenant breaking acts. *If... ye will not do all My commandments, but that ye break My covenant: I also will do this unto you;* ***I will even appoint over you terror*** (Leviticus 26:14-16 KJV). God is in charge; He gives certain events *for a sign and for a wonder* so we would know He is judging us (Deuteronomy 28:46 KJV).

Just weeks after the Democrats and Republicans prayed with false gods at the 2016 national conventions, three Muslim terrorist attacks occurred within a 12 hour period. First, the Minnesota Mall stabbings, with 8 people wounded. Then the New York City and New Jersey bombings that injured 29 more people.[6] Then there was the brutal Ohio State Muslim terrorist attack.

Afterwards, the Ft. Lauderdale airport terrorist shootings by an Islamic convert killed five people and wounded six others. This happened after the announcement that false gods would be included by those planning inauguration events for Trump. While we want to end terrorism, the Holy Bible says that no amount of money or military strikes will make it go away until we obey God's Word and repent of covenant breaking acts against God, as this book explains how to do.

Does God Speak Through Donald Trump?

Be encouraged for God is causing Trump to work to end many judgments on the nation, even with some of the President's tweets. God is using the President to secure the open borders, bring jobs back that were lost to other countries, and to keep the USA's wealth for Americans.

Foreigners flooding in are God's judgment. ***The gates of thy land shall be set wide open unto thine enemies*** (Nahum 3:13 KJV). We saw this when Obama and Congress brought in terrorists, gangs, those with contagious diseases, and millions of people who oppose our Christian nation. God doesn't say to let everyone into the USA. While God is love, He is just and only allows in Heaven those who follow Jesus Christ (John 14:6). Losing jobs and multiple languages is a Biblical curse from our sins. ***The foreigner that is within you shall get up above you very high; and you shall come down very low*** (Deuteronomy 28:43 KJV).

Did God speak through Trump while campaigning to end this judgment and to protect the USA? *Donald J. Trump is calling for a total and complete shutdown of Muslims entering the United States until our country's representatives can figure out what is going on. According to Pew Research, among others, there is great hatred towards Americans by large segments of the Muslim population. Most recently, a poll from the Center for Security Policy released data showing "25% of those polled agreed that violence against Americans here in the*

United States is justified as a part of the global jihad" and 51% of those polled, "agreed that Muslims in America should have the choice of being governed according to Shariah." Shariah authorizes such atrocities as murder against non-believers who won't convert, beheadings and more unthinkable acts that pose great harm to Americans, especially women. [7]

God wants us to avoid a financial collapse and to have better jobs. But in judgment, the country's money has been plundered by spoilers. They *rejected His statutes, and His covenant that He made with their fathers... they... went after the heathen... and worshipped all the host of heaven... they caused their sons and their daughters to pass through the fire, and used divination...* ***Therefore the LORD... delivered them into the hand of spoilers*** (2 Kings 17:15-20 KJV).

Did we hear God's mercy to end this judgment in President Trump's inauguration speech? He said, *"[we] spent trillions of dollars overseas... We've made other countries rich while the wealth, strength, and confidence of our country has disappeared over the horizon. One by one, the factories shuttered and left our shores..."* God is using Trump to help Americans and to stop the spoiling of the nation's wealth.

Yet, if our nation won't follow the Bible, there will be hard times, jobs will be lost, and enemies may invade us. But if we obey God, there will be Biblical prosperity.

Our Nation's Troubles Are Caused By Sin

We see that schools have fallen to the point where they indoctrinate children with sin, including strange gods, sex before marriage, abortion, and the lies of evolution. They also have removed the plethora of facts about our nation being dedicated to God from the lessons. We must save our children's souls from these lies and the danger of hell.

The life we know is at risk if we don't defend Christianity. God's people have been attacked by those who hate Jesus Christ. As you may have heard, Christian florists, bakers, clerks, and workers have been unjustly fired, jailed, or fined for following God. In Alabama, highly respected Judge Roy Moore, who believes in traditional marriage, was unjustly suspended from being Chief Justice.[8] Kim Davis, a county clerk in Kentucky, was unfairly and wrongly jailed for following her conscience to oppose same-sex marriage.[9]

While we have restored some of God's favor, the country can't be exceptional until there is more repentance of the sins causing God's judgment and Biblical curses. Sin affects our safety, strength, and prosperity, so it must be addressed across the nation, in churches and dinner conversations. God's judgment comes from the people opposing Him with:

- False gods
- Homosexuality, adultery, and fornication
- Not calling for Christian religious liberty
- Not standing up for our God-given rights
- Rebellion to God's sovereignty in our government
- Helping the ungodly in politics and business
- Abortion
- Coveting (wanting other people's items, greed)
- The occult, sorcery, and witchcraft

How can our lives truly improve without ending these harmful ways? How can we say we are friends of God if we act against Him as an enemy? To make the USA great again, we must search our hearts, see if there are any sins to turn from, and have national repentance of all wickedness.

Who Makes America Great?

The good news is: God gives us a way out. The secret to life is Jesus Christ. He gets us and the USA right with God, as the *one mediator between God and men* (1 Timothy 2:5 KJV). Who is the light of the world? Jesus. Without Him we live in darkness and lies. Without Him we can do nothing. Through Him come all blessings for our lives and the USA.

History affirms, America is great because **Jesus Makes:**

- **America Safe** - God protects those who are in covenant with Him. There is no safety for ourselves, children, and loved ones outside of God (Psalm 91).
- **America Prosperous** - When we seek first the Kingdom of God and His righteousness all things are added to us (Matthew 6:33).
- **America Free** - Jesus is the author of liberty. There is no freedom without Him, because men and nations are naturally slaves to sin and to the prince of the world. Jesus is the one who sets us free from tyranny, communism, Shariah Law, and the New World Order.
- **America Strong** - God gives strength to those who rely on Him. *The LORD is my rock, and my fortress, and my deliverer; my God, my strength, in whom I will trust* (Psalm 18:2 KJV). *Except the LORD keep the city, the watchman wakes but in vain* (Psalm 127:1 KJV).

- **Education Great** - America's Schoolmaster, Noah Webster, said, *Without the Bible education is useless.*[10]
- **Families Great** - A home can only have Christian love and a foundation in God by Jesus Christ.
- **Americans Wise** - *The fear of the LORD is the beginning of knowledge: but fools despise wisdom and instruction* (Proverbs 1:7 KJV).
- **Americans Dream Big** - The USA has a holy motive with God and *with God all things are possible* (Mark 10:27 KJV).
- **America the Home of the Brave** - By following Jesus, we are "the land of the free and the home of the brave". Francis Scott Key, who wrote our national anthem said, "seek to establish for his country... such a character... not unworthy of the name of a Christian nation."[11]
- **America Win** - The greatest thing we can do as a nation is God's will. That is real winning. True American patriots dedicated to the will of God won the Revolutionary War for our Christian liberty.

Our goal is to please God. He wants a covenant Christian nation that loves Him and does His will. This is what our founders gave us, so we must faithfully keep covenant. It is why God raised the USA up to be the preeminent nation. Jesus Christ is the only one who can make your life and America great. He is the only way we have to be right with God. Any other way won't work. How can being lukewarm about God or opposing Him be honorable or fruitful?

The Bible teaches the secret to God's favor is:

- Americans serve the LORD, not false gods.
- Americans seek God with all our heart and soul.

- Americans obey the Holy Bible, with the LORD as our lawgiver and judge.
- Americans have no king but King Jesus.
- Americans make disciples of the USA.
- Americans turn away from everything against Jesus Christ.
- The USA acknowledging the Cross and receiving forgiveness through Jesus Christ for our personal and national sins.

Think about it: Does God consider a country great that goes against the Holy Bible—such as communist and Hindu societies? Do the people in China or India really have better lives than those in America? The answer is "No." Without Jesus, people are lost in darkness and despair.

We see this fact evidenced in various ways: The hopelessness of communist tyranny and the poverty of the lower castes in polytheistic India. In contrast, Christianity is what gives safety and liberty to America.

The Bible says only those who follow Jesus Christ are forgiven by His blood for their sins, have the Holy Spirit, walk in God's love, have wisdom, and do God's will. The people following Jesus make the USA extraordinary.

What do the founding fathers, who made America great, reveal to us? By their words and actions, our forefathers:

- Made the USA's top priority to be Christian religious liberty to serve the LORD freely.
- Consecrated the USA to God in covenant.

It is urgent we follow our Christian founders, because our personal and national destinies are at stake, including:

- Happiness or suffering
- Christian liberty or persecution

- Financial prosperity or economic collapse
- Strong families or broken homes
- Peace or wars
- Life or death
- Americanism or globalism

The way we follow Jesus to make the USA great again is by re-affirming covenant. This is accomplished by doing *7 Specific Bible Truths* that we will now learn. They are God's commands for us. If you will re-affirm covenant, then you are a modern day American hero restoring safety and prosperity.

We and our churches must quickly follow the step-by-step Biblical plan in **JESUS MAKES AMERICA GREAT.** Every blessing in our nation's history has come from what we will discover. We can expect continuous American breakthroughs because of following Jesus Christ.

Prayer

Father, You are merciful. We humble ourselves, get on our knees, and declare, Jesus makes America great for Your glory. In Jesus' name. Amen.

Reflection Questions

1. *What did our founders do to make America great?*
2. *According to the Word of God, what sins result in invasion, captivity, or destruction?*
3. *Why does Jesus make America great? Explain.*

2
First Truth—
Covenant with the True God

The first act of Congress - George Washington, John Adams, Samuel Adams, and our Founding Fathers praying in Jesus' name and reading the Holy Bible in 1774. Washington (center), John Adams (sixth from top left) and Samuel Adams (left of John Adams in light coat).

"Blessed is the nation whose God is the LORD..."

Psalm 33:12 KJV

America is the most amazing story of God orchestrating the details of the USA. If your school didn't censor it, you know the Jamestown Settlers' first act was to pray, fast, plant a cross on the Virginia beach, and covenant America to God "to all generations." The first permanent English settlers consecrated America to God forever. **Our covenant from 1607** says:

We do hereby dedicate this Land, and ourselves, to reach the People within these shores with the Gospel of Jesus Christ, and to raise up Godly generations after us, and with these generations take the Kingdom of God to all the earth. May this Covenant of Dedication remain to all generations, as long as this earth remains, and may this Land... be Evangelist to the World. May all who see this Cross, remember what we have done here, and may those who come here to inhabit join us in this Covenant...[1] (Jamestown Settlers, 1607).

The Pilgrims' covenant love for God also gives us hope. The Mayflower Compact reveals our country is God's nation:

IN THE NAME OF GOD, AMEN... Having undertaken for the Glory of God, and Advancement of the Christian Faith... Do by these Presents, solemnly and mutually, in the Presence of God and one another, covenant and combine ourselves together into a civil Body Politick... Anno Domini; 1620.[2]

The Puritans arrived in 1630. Famous John Winthrop wrote, *We are entered into covenant with Him for this work.*[3]

The true American dream is stated with the New England Confederation in 1643. It reminds us that *we all came into these parts of America with one and the same end and aim, namely, to advance the Kingdom of our Lord Jesus Christ and to enjoy the liberties of the Gospel in purity with peace.*[4] Nothing is more American than Christian religious liberty!

Congress Pledged the USA's Allegiance to God

A small group of faithful men, young and old, were united in silent submission to humbly seek God's deliverance and protection. They understood that His will was for our nation to freely follow Jesus Christ. The decisions that our First Continental Congress made, based on the study of the Bible and prayer to our Christian God, would lead to events creating a document that would change the course of millions of lives centuries into the future, including yours.

The birth of the Declaration of Independence two years later, one of the most important documents in history, was derived from such acts of prayer. This simple, yet courageous show of loyalty to obey God instead of man would bring the greatest levels of Christian freedom ever seen, with unprecedented blessings to all who follow in agreement.

The first act of Congress occurred when our founding fathers humbled themselves and sought God. Walking in covenant gave them the bold confidence to petition Him for deliverance from tyranny as they laid the foundations for self-government built upon Jesus Christ. Yet, as we saw our nation's covenant begins much earlier, with the settlers consecrating our nation to God as the first act of America.

The forefathers confirm the USA's priority is to follow Jesus. The Bible and history show that following the Son of God results in God's safety, power, and prosperity for us.

Motivated to make disciples, our founders taught all children the Bible and Christian prayer in schools. In covenant George Washington assured Delaware Indian chiefs, *I am glad you have brought three of the children of your principal chiefs to be educated with us... You do well to wish to learn... above all, the religion of Jesus Christ. These will make you a greater and happier people than you are. Congress will do everything they can to assist you in this wise intention.*[5]

The USA is more superior than a nation of Christians, for if one person is in covenant, God honors our covenant. The Supreme Court said, *This is a Christian nation.*[6]

Boldly the Pledge of Allegiance testifies that our country is a Christian Republic with the phrase, *to the Republic for which it stands, one nation under God.* Which God? The LORD.

The USA's God Is The LORD

Our forefathers making the LORD our God is significant, because He is the one true God. *I am the first, and I am the last; and beside me there is no God* (Isaiah 44:6 KJV).

Our founders knew of three remarkable Bible accounts of God's covenant mercy. These are found with Kings Asa and Josiah, and Moses (2 Chronicles 15 and 34, Exodus 32).

With riots, divisions, and terrorists, there is some similarity for us to King Asa's day when there was no peace... nation was destroyed of nation, and city of city (2 Chronicles 15:5-6 KJV). But Asa found hope that God was with Judah while they were with Him; and if they sought Him, He would be found. God would free them of the trouble. Asa knew the LORD was righteous and if they weren't with God, He wouldn't be with them (2 Chronicles 15:2).

King Josiah lived in a time where the Word of God was set aside and forgotten. He loved God, so to honor the LORD he commissioned the repairing of God's temple. Suddenly the

Law of God was found in the recesses of the temple and the priests brought it to the king. For the first time in his life Josiah heard these words and saw the connection between the nation's sins and God's judgment. Seeing that God's judgment was on Judah, he tore his clothes in desperation and fear. He ordered the false gods to be destroyed and led the people to serve the LORD and turn from evil.

When Josiah inquired of God, he discovered their lives were in jeopardy for forsaking God and said, *great is the wrath of the LORD that is poured out upon us, because our fathers have not kept the word of the LORD* (2 Chronicles 34:21 KJV). So King Josiah and the people renewed covenant to live for the LORD and a great revival came.

We must have a tender heart of love for God and reaffirm covenant. Amazingly, revival came after evil King Manasseh forgot God. There is always hope. God's favor returned when the people showed God they loved Him and *entered into a covenant to seek the LORD God of their fathers with all their heart and with all their soul* (2 Chronicles 15:12 KJV).

First Bible Truth to make the USA great *Psalm 33:12, 2 Cor. 6:16*	**Re-affirm Covenant: The LORD is the God of the USA and Americans are His people** *Why? To get our nation in right relationship with God.*

The only way to be blessed is to make the one true God our God. *Blessed is the nation whose God is the LORD; and the people whom he hath chosen for his own inheritance.* (Psalm

33:12 KJV). The opposite is true. The people who don't declare the LORD is the USA's God curse the nation.

The First Bible Truth to make the USA great again is to re-affirm covenant the USA's God is the LORD. This American breakthrough secret assures that God will make our nation great and restore His kind blessings to our lives, making Americans (those in covenant) God's special people. By doing this, we are in right relationship with God and are not His enemy. It is helpful to remember the Bible teaches the world is God's enemy (James 4:4).

The USA Is a Christian Nation Forever

We know God wants covenant nations, as Israel proves. No other nation has the same covenant with Jesus Christ that the USA has. We are unique and must protect our covenant. Having great wisdom, our founders understood that our nation could be God's people through the New Covenant of Jesus Christ, which is for whosoever believes. It is a "better covenant" than the Old Covenant (Hebrews 8:6 KJV).

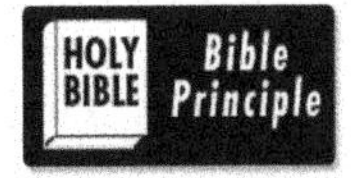

Our founders show how a few people can make the strongest Christian nation.

Those who disagree are the people causing God's judgment, because to say America is no longer a Christian nation is a covenant breaking act. Consider Judah. Was the country no longer a covenant nation to the LORD when King Manasseh and the people did so much evil? At least one person was faithful to

God. Thus when King Josiah took reign, the nation followed God. That is where some people miss it. Are you no longer a Christian if you fall into sin? As long as you hold onto Jesus, which is holding onto covenant, you are a Christian. *For a just man falleth seven times, and riseth up again* (Proverbs 24:16 KJV).

It is unwise to listen to Obama and those outside of our covenant. Their words have no meaning. David never paid attention to Goliath, who was not in covenant.

Sadly, some Christians criticize our founders. But have those dishonoring our forefathers risked their life for the USA to break free from tyranny to follow God? Do they say America belongs to Jesus Christ? Will they declare to our country their "abhorrence and detestation" of homosexual sin as George Washington did?[9] We are to honor our founders.

We know how to stop losing the war on terror. Terrorism is defeated by: (1) Covenant acts that the LORD is the God of the USA and (2) Our nation obeying the Bible (Leviticus 26:14-16). To protect our loved ones, declare *Jesus Christ is Lord of the USA*. We have good news. The *7 Bible Truths* are guaranteed by God to end terror.

God Gives Protection, Abundance, and Blessings

As a nation, we have seen more of heaven on earth than those living in any other country. The USA is historically known for blessed lives, wisdom, godly behavior, and Christian freedom, because of these covenant acts. Americans have secure futures. No other nation compares to the USA.

America has stood above all other nations in prosperity. Higher employment rates, better jobs, and the dollar having greater value come by our nation making Jesus our priority.[7,8]

We have happier lives when the USA puts our Lord first. More people stay married. Children are better educated and have less troubles when taught the Bible in school, because the Holy Spirit fills their lives with wisdom, understanding, and knowledge (Proverbs 1). Our family and friends are more likely to go to heaven by trusting in Jesus for their salvation when the government promotes the Gospel as our founders did. Christians are honored and not persecuted. The whole nation is safer.

Additional blessings that come by rallying together and defending Christianity as a nation are:

- Following Jesus Christ is what makes the USA one of God's greatest assets on earth
- Protecting Christians
- National sovereignty and unity
- The best leaders
- Freedom from a police state (i.e. the militarization of the police force, restricting free speech, martial law...)
- Ridding our country of corruption
- National security from God and peace for the people

Will You Choose the LORD for the USA's God?

We are a Christian Republic, with God as our sovereign. Then under God we the people are next sovereign. That is why Americans do not believe in a ruling political class.

Our forefathers say Jesus is sovereign above all government (Psalm 2). John Hancock led the people with, *The great and most important Blessing, the Gospel of Jesus Christ... that all may bow to the scepter of our LORD JESUS CHRIST...*[10]

Will you join covenant by agreeing the USA's God is the one true God? This lets Him know that you and the USA are on His side, which means safety, strength, liberty, prosperity, and the defeat of our enemies. Just reject all other gods since they cause harm and declare, *The LORD is my God and I am His.*

Since the LORD is our God and He is good, we thank, praise, and worship Him. This is part of having the LORD be our God. Everyday we magnify Him by saying things like, "I and the USA exalt You LORD." He is worthy!

As we glorify Him, He defeats our enemies (2 Chronicles 20). That is why agreeing that the USA serves the true God gives us national security. For our protection, all churches should hold services re-affirming the USA serves the LORD.

If you read the *Harbinger* book, you probably wanted to know what to do next. These powerful *7 Bible Truths* are the solution to the *Harbinger*, which is from the Isaiah 9:10 analogy of the bricks falling and the sycamore tree being cut down. God's answer for America's future is found on another tree—the more significant tree at Calvary. Four verses before we find God's remedy of Jesus Christ, *the government shall be upon His shoulder* (Isaiah 9:6 KJV); the cross at Calvary gives us mercy and grace. Everything is restored by Jesus.

Those who won't renounce strange gods are the ones who endanger the country. However, all who make the decision to follow the one true God make the USA great.

Next, we learn valuable, true American secrets.

Prayer

Father, You, LORD, are the God of the USA
and Americans are Your people.
In Jesus' name. Amen.

Reflection Questions

1. *Christians serve a different God than other people. Explain why the LORD is the one true God.*
2. *Why does God's favor come to you when you renounce all other gods?*
3. *Read Psalm 33:12. Will you publicly say the LORD is the God of the USA? Why?*
4. *How could the faith of only a few first Christian settlers make the greatest Christian nation ever?*

3

American Secrets for Safe and Blessed Lives

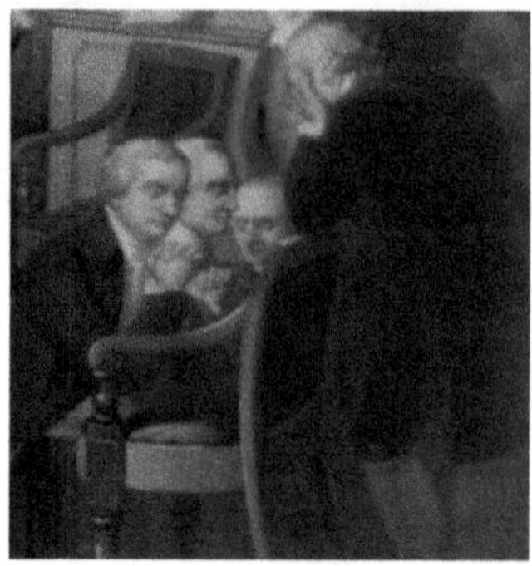

The founding fathers seeking God in Congress. John Jay, first Chief Justice, is second from left.

"The secret of the LORD is with them that fear him; and he will shew them his covenant."
Psalm 25:14 KJV

Americans have stood far above all other nations with God's protection, freedom, and abundance. So, let's answer: What are the next things our founders did to attain these special blessings? How can we do the same?

There are *American Secrets* that honor God as first place in everything for our nation. They are a key foundation for the *7 Bible Truths* and are core beliefs of the famed pastors and Christians who founded America. Much of the corruption has been because these mature Christian beliefs have been missing from many churches, who only teach basic Christianity, which does not produce America. Following these secrets makes our churches great again.

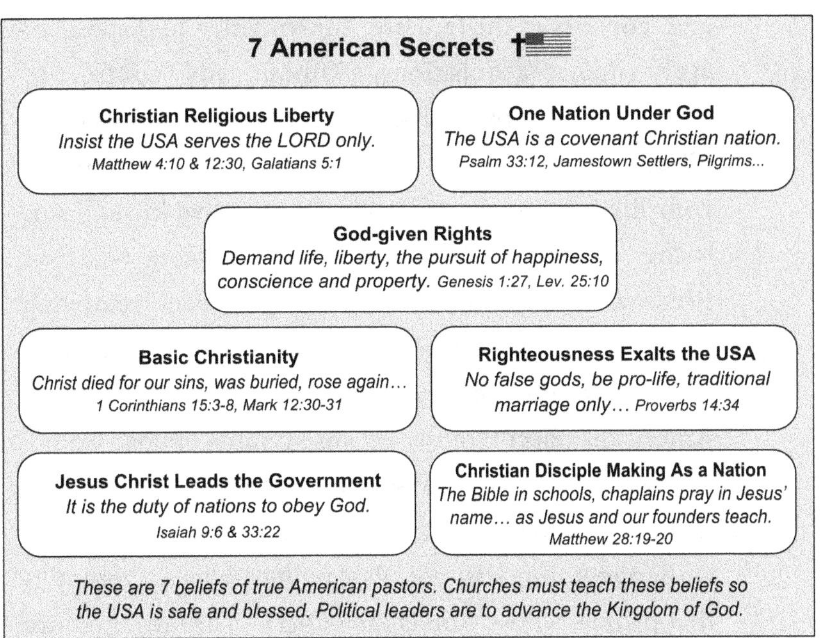

7 American Secrets
Christian Religious Liberty
Insist the USA serves the LORD only.
Matthew 4:10 & 12:30, Galatians 5:1
One Nation Under God
The USA is a covenant Christian nation.
Psalm 33:12, Jamestown Settlers, Pilgrims...
God-given Rights
Demand life, liberty, the pursuit of happiness, conscience and property. Genesis 1:27, Lev. 25:10
Basic Christianity
Christ died for our sins, was buried, rose again...
1 Corinthians 15:3-8, Mark 12:30-31
Righteousness Exalts the USA
No false gods, be pro-life, traditional marriage only... Proverbs 14:34
Jesus Christ Leads the Government
It is the duty of nations to obey God.
Isaiah 9:6 & 33:22
Christian Disciple Making As a Nation
The Bible in schools, chaplains pray in Jesus' name... as Jesus and our founders teach.
Matthew 28:19-20
These are 7 beliefs of true American pastors. Churches must teach these beliefs so the USA is safe and blessed. Political leaders are to advance the Kingdom of God.

Your rights come from God, not man (Acts 5:29). The Declaration of Independence says, *all men are endowed by their Creator with certain unalienable rights, among these are life, liberty, and the pursuit of happiness.* Government can't take away rights. That is why Americans demand our God-given rights. Man is made in the image of God (Genesis 1:27).

Your unalienable rights are to live for God, and include:

- **Life:** You have the right to life in all you do, beginning at conception. In Jesus is life, so this right is to follow Him. The Bible says, *In Him was life; and the life was* *the light of men* (John 1:4 KJV). "Life is the immediate gift of God, a right inherent by Nature [God's creation] in every individual and it begins in contemplation of law as soon as an infant is able to stir in the mother's womb" and "consists in the free use, enjoyment, and disposal of every man's acquisitions, without any control or diminution,"[1] explained scholar Sir William Blackstone.

- **Liberty:** Your right of liberty includes freedom to live your life for God as a Christian, not to live in sin. Jesus is the Author of Liberty and only He makes you free. Personal liberty "consists in the power of removing one's person to any place whatsoever without restraint, unless by due course of law," said Blackstone.[2] Americans reject tyranny because tyrants oppose God.
- **The Pursuit of happiness:** Your right to the pursuit of happiness is to do God's will, for you are created to only be happy doing His will. Psalm 144:15 says, "Happy is that people, whose God is the LORD." The law of nature (the will of God) forbids doing things gainst another person's pursuit of happiness. Jesus commanded to love your neighbor as yourself (Mark 12:31).
- **Property:** You have the right to property. This includes using your property to glorify God. *The earth is the LORD's, and the fullness thereof* (Psalm 24:1 KJV). A person's right of private property "consists in the free use, enjoyment, and disposal of all his acquisitions, without any control or diminution, save only by the [Christian] laws of the land," explained Blackstone.[3]

- **Conscience:** Your right of conscience is the duty to obey your conscience before God in holiness (Acts 5:29). The Bible teaches that no one can force you to sin. A person who tries to force you to sin is evil.

The LORD gives us God-given rights to be holy, He does not give us rights to sin. This means that "homosexual, rights," "abortion rights" and other sins are Satan-given rights.

We must only stand up for Christian religious liberty to serve the LORD, not religious liberty of false gods. The reason is so we don't provoke God (2 Chronicles 34:25).

Our Christian founders typically use the word "religion" to mean Christianity, since the King James Version of the Bible does this (James 1:26-27). When we read our founders saying "religious liberty," they often mean "Christian liberty". To prove this, they put the Bible in schools, not other beliefs. That is why the media, politicians, ministers, and those who say "freedom of all religions" put the nation in great risk.

To help other gods is dangerous. If Moses had said, "Israel must have liberty for Baal and also the LORD," God could have killed Moses for forsaking Him (Exodus 32). When Aaron sinned with the molten calf, Moses reminds us, *the LORD was very angry with Aaron to have destroyed him* (Deuteronomy 9:20 KJV). God is holy. As our Creator and Judge, He calls the USA to worship Him only, not strange gods. It is a covenant breaking act to help false religions. If you have aided other gods, confess this sin and be forgiven.

The purpose of government is to serve Jesus Christ (Isaiah 9:6). That is why Justice Joseph Story famously explained **the First Amendment is for Christianity**, not to approve of non-Christian beliefs. Law students studied Story's popular "Commentaries on the Constitution" from 1833 to 1905. It explains: *The real object of the [First] Amendment was, not to countenance [approve], much less to advance Mohammedanism, or Judaism, or infidelity [secularism], by prostrating Christianity, but to exclude all rivalry among Christian sects, and to prevent any national ecclesiastical establishment [denomination], which should give to an hierarchy the exclusive patronage of the national government.*[4]

Our founders prayed in Jesus' name, read the Bible in government, and wrote the Constitution. Laws against Christians and our conscience are illegal. **The First Amendment means:** *Congress [because its rights are limited] shall make no law respecting an establishment of [one Christian denomination] religion, or prohibiting the free exercise [of Christianity] thereof...*

Christians wrote our Christian Constitution for Christians. The Constitution:

(1) Begins with "blessings".

(2) Prevents Congress from making a law prohibiting the free exercise of Christianity in the First Amendment.

(3) Includes "Sundays excepted" to honor the Lord in Article 1, Section 7.

(4) Ends with "in the Year of our Lord" to affirm Jesus Christ is Lord of the USA.

(5) Has Bible principles throughout it and it is based on our Christian Declaration of Independence.

We know God's favor to the USA is from Christians, not unbelievers. Our founders taught school children, *Almost all civil liberty... owes its origin to the principles of the Christian religion. Men began to understand their natural rights, as soon as the reformation from popery began to dawn in the sixteenth century... to this we owe our free constitutions of government.*[5]

America Is Above All Nations

God's secrets of America reveal key reasons why He favors the USA. The *7 Bible Truths* and these secrets, which are part of the first Bible Truth, are why America stands out.

Next, we learn how to find God and to have His help to make our lives and nation extraordinary.

Prayer

Father, the USA exalts Jesus Christ.
Give every Christian boldness to demand to
have Christian religious liberty.
In Jesus' name. Amen.

Reflection Questions

1. *How does righteousness exalt a nation? Explain.*
2. *Why does saying "freedom of all religions" anger God?*
3. *Explain each of your God-given rights.*

4

Second Truth—Seek and Find God

George Washington praying to the LORD God.

"They entered into a covenant to seek the LORD God of their fathers with all their heart and with all their soul;"
2 Chronicles 15:12 KJV

George Washington kneels in desperation searching for answers. As commander in chief, all he could do at this point was seek the true Commander in Chief, our Lord. His men were sick, hungry, and cold. He had sought help earnestly from men, but it wasn't enough. So as he often did, he knelt to seek God's help at Valley Forge.

Seeking God Gives His Help and Answers

The Second Bible Truth is seeking God with all our heart and all our soul means we find Him and have His help. We go from living in risk to finding God's wisdom and mighty deliverance.

Second Bible Truth to make the USA great *2 Chron. 15:12, Matt. 7:7*	**Seek God with all your heart and all your soul** *Why? To find God and His help.*

Seeking God is the only way to do great things. We seek God so we do His will. If we don't seek God, then we do mediocre and sinful things. To seek God is to wholeheartedly look for Him, to know His will, and to find His help about fixing our nation's problems. Finding God's answer is knowing how to save our nation, instead of having false hope.

When Judah humbled themselves to make covenant in Asa's time, the people were happy to seek God and end their problems. *Judah rejoiced at the oath: for they had sworn with all their heart, and sought Him with their whole desire; and He was found of them: and the LORD gave them rest round about* (2 Chronicles 15:15 KJV). Judah was not destroyed in Josiah's life because God saw Josiah humble himself (2 Kings 22:19).

There is much to learn and gain by seeking God. Jesus promises, *Ask, and it shall be given you; seek, and ye shall find; knock, and it shall be opened unto you* (Matthew 7:7 KJV).

When you seek God:

- **You find God:** *Thou shalt find him, if thou seek him with all thy heart and with all thy soul.* (Deut. 4:29 KJV)

- **The LORD helps you:** *For You, LORD, have not forsaken those who seek You.* (Psalm 9:10 KJV)
- **God rewards you:** *But without faith it is impossible to please Him, for he who comes to God must believe that He is, and that He is a rewarder of those who diligently seek Him.* (Hebrews 11:6 KJV)
- **You prosper:** *As long as he sought the LORD, God made him to prosper.* (2 Chronicles 26:5 KJV)
- **You have all you need:** *They that seek the LORD shall not want any good thing.* (Psalm 34:10 KJV)
- **You do God's work:** *Now set your heart and your soul to seek the LORD your God; arise therefore, and build.* (2 Chronicles 12:14 KJV)
- **You have life:** *Your heart shall live* that seek God.* (Psalm 69:32 KJV) *The word "live" means to have life, live prosperously, and to be restored to health.
- **You avoid evil:** *He did evil, because he prepared not his heart to seek the LORD.* (2 Chronicles 12:14 KJV)
- **You understand all things:** *They that seek the LORD understand all things.* (Proverbs 28:5 KJV)

How to Seek God for the USA

Our nation seeking God is especially important. Let's look at a couple examples from Scripture.

Moses knew God because He sought God. Recall, when Israel turned to the molten calf and forsook the LORD, God saw this sin as a covenant breaking act. He said to Moses, *let me alone, that my wrath may wax hot against them, and that I may consume them* (Exodus 32:10 KJV). However, God allowed Moses to remind Him of covenant with Israel. Then Moses separated the people by finding out who loved God and who didn't by asking: Who is on the LORD'S side? (Exodus 32:10-26 KJV). If Moses had not sought God, all the people might have died.

When Israel suffered a famine, King David sought God and learned what sin caused judgment. *The LORD answered, It is for Saul, and for his bloody house, because he slew the Gibeonites* (2 Samuel 21:1 KJV). The Gibeonites lived in Israel's promised land and were to be destroyed. But they lied to Israel and Israel made a treaty because they didn't seek God (Joshua 9). Then, when Saul went against Joshua's words, God judged them. But David found the answer to stop judgment!

I hope that you are optimistic because doing these *Bible Truths* will bring back jobs for Americans and give us peace not war. Following God's blueprint will save millions of souls, heal marriages, free our nation from communist threats, and have Christians honored in schools and at work again.

To help our nation seek the LORD, here are some questions that we and our churches can prayerfully ask:

- Will this act bring God's blessings or judgment?
- Does this decision bring Americans closer to God?
- How can the USA's sins be forgiven?
- Why does God forbid America to have other gods?
- If we do this will more go to Heaven or hell?
- What qualifications does God have for leaders?
- How does the Bible say to drain the swamp of political corruption?
- Will this choice make us more heavenly or worldly?
- What national sins can we repent of?

God has the answers we are searching for.

George Washington and his men made it through that difficult winter in Valley Forge defending our freedom because he humbled himself before the true Commander in Chief and found Him. God faithfully answered his prayer. Even though the army was weakened, they were able to claim a resounding win! Eventually God gave us complete victory and independence since Americans kept seeking Him.

Will you turn to God with all your heart and soul? If so, you are on His side. Have faith! He always rewards the USA for seeking Him. Victory and miracles happen!

The next *Bible Truth* reveals how to do God's will.

Prayer

Here is a prayer to seek God as a nation:

Father,

Americans love You—You are the USA's God and we are Your people. With all our heart and soul, we seek You to:

- *Mercifully end Your judgment.*
- *Lead our country. The USA submits to You.*
- *Give us Christian leaders who fear You for school boards, city, state, and federal government.*
- *Lead Americans not into temptation. Deliver the USA from evil (everything against You).*
- *Teach us if __ will make our nation holy, or unholy.*
- *Show Americans what Your Word says about __.*

- *We trust in You to protect the USA from all enemies foreign and domestic.*

Americans thank and praise You. In Jesus' name. Amen.

 Reflection Questions

1. *Why does seeking God protect our lives? Explain.*
2. *How often do you seek God in the decisions you make?*
3. *In what ways can you be like King Asa and King Josiah in seeking God with all your heart and all your soul? What are some things you will do?*
4. *How can your church seek God for the USA? In what ways? How often?*

5

Third Truth—Live the Bible Way

"To keep His commandments... with all his heart, and with all his soul, to perform the words of the covenant which are written in this book."
2 Chronicles 34:31 KJV

Jesus Christ is the Word of God. This is an important reason why we stand in awe of God's Word. God says, *In the beginning was the Word, and the Word was with God, and the Word was God* and *His name is called The Word of God* (John 1:1, Revelation 19:13 KJV).

When King Josiah and Judah found the Word of God that their fathers lost, the people followed God. They *made a covenant before the LORD, to walk after the LORD, and to keep his commandments...* (2 Chronicles 34:31 KJV). Living for God saved their lives. Like Judah found the book of the law, we are learning from the Word of God these *7 Bible Truths* that safeguard our lives and homes.

The LORD Is Our Lawgiver

The Third Bible Truth to make the USA great is obedience to the Word of God assures that God will protect our lives and nation, gives us wisdom, and makes the economy strong. Safety comes by obeying God's Word. This is because we do His will. To obey God goes with the *Second Bible Truth* to seek and find Him, since part of seeking Him is to learn what He says. This is living the Bible way. To love God is to do what He says and this make the nation remarkable. We do the greatest work possible by obeying the Bible.

Third Bible Truth to make the USA great *Luke 6:47-49, 2 Chron. 34:31*	**Obey the Holy Bible** **with all your heart and all your soul** *Why? To do God's will.*

To have justice, we must affirm the Bible is God's revealed law. It is our duty to obey our Creator or we face consequences. *The doctrines thus delivered we call the revealed or divine law, and they are to be found only in the Holy Scriptures,*[1] taught legal scholar Sir William Blackstone.

Who makes our laws? The Bible says, *the LORD is our lawgiver* (Isaiah 33:22 KJV). To do God's will, our founders established that our laws are from Scripture. With wisdom they made Christian laws and expect us to keep them, including to honor God by traditional marriage. This is because the Bible is the bedrock of the USA's legal system.

The Supreme Court affirmed, *It is well known that for our present form of government we are greatly indebted to his*

[Justice James Wilson's] exertions and influence... he states that profaneness and blasphemy [of God] are offences punishable by fine and imprisonment, and that Christianity is part of the common law.[1] Wilson signed both the Declaration of Independence and the Constitution; George Washington appointed him to the original Supreme Court.

Human law must rest its authority, ultimately, upon the authority of that law, which is divine,[2] taught Justice Wilson, as the first law professor at the University of Pennsylvania.

By acknowledging God is our lawgiver, you bring justice to the USA and remove corruption. So praying a prayer like this makes a difference, "Father, You reign. I only recognize Your laws. I thank You that You are filling the USA with Your laws right now. In Jesus' name. Amen." Then publicly stand up and say, "The LORD is our lawgiver; He only blesses laws that are based on the Bible."

The Bible's Five Requirements for Leaders

America is great because of choosing Christian leaders. Here are God's requirements for leaders:

1. **Able Christians Who Fear God** *Exodus 18:21, 2 Cor. 6:14-18*
   - They know the LORD is our Judge, Lawgiver, and King, so they follow the Holy Bible (Isaiah 33:22).
   - Their goal is the true American Dream of advancing the Kingdom of our Lord Jesus Christ.
   - Obeying God, they are pro-life and for traditional marriage only, and call for schools to daily read the Bible and have Christian prayer (Matthew 5:21, 2 Peter 2:6, Isaiah 59:21).

- As Jesus Christ serves the church, they serve Americans (Luke 22:26).
- They believe that our national security is first *In God We Trust (*Mark 12:31, Psalm 121:1 & 146:3-5).
- They have a Biblical view of the USA's war policy, which is defensive (just cause) non-aggressive wars. If in war, they call to quickly win the war.

2. **Call for Christian Religious Liberty** *Mark 12:30, Gal. 5:1*
   - Following God, they boldly stand up to have Christian religious liberty throughout the USA (Matthew 4:10).
   - They understand that the Constitution was written by Christians to protect Christians to serve the LORD.
3. **Insist to Have God-given Rights** *Genesis 1:27, Acts 5:29*
   - Since our rights are endowed by our Creator and can never be surrendered, they affirm our Biblical rights.
   - They are known for defending our unalienable rights of life, liberty, the pursuit of happiness, property, and conscience.
4. **Truthful** *Exodus 18:21*
   - They are known for honesty not lying.
   - They condemn all unconstitutional acts, so they don't limit our rights, but they limit government's power.
5. **Hate Covetousness** *Exodus 8:21*
   - They refuse to take what belongs to *We the People.*
   - With verifiable histories, they prove that they are effective at eliminating unjust taxes and cutting debts.
   - As the Bible teaches, they promote self-government.

Prosperity Comes By Obeying God's Word

Doing God's will, which is to do what the Bible teaches, causes blessings to come to you and the USA and makes our way prosperous. Jesus said, *seek ye first the kingdom of God, and his righteousness; and all these things shall be added unto you.* (Matthew 6:33 KJV). Look at these verses and see why and how God promises to prosper us:

- "If thou shalt hearken diligently unto the voice of the LORD thy God, to observe and to do all his commandments... the LORD thy God will set thee on high above all nations of the earth: And all these blessings shall come on thee... (Deut. 28:1-2 KJV)
- " This book of the law shall not depart out of thy mouth; but thou shalt meditate therein day and night, that thou mayest observe to do according to all that is written therein: for then thou shalt make thy way prosperous, and then thou shalt have good success." (Joshua 1:8 KJV)

We are always to love God, not money—even after God blesses us financially and with wealth. *For the love of money is the root of all evil* (1 Timothy 6:10 KJV). No one wants to forget God. So, let's make sure we put Him first in every part of our lives every day. An easy check that confirms God is our priority is to see if we are following all *7 Bible Truths.*

The Bible Is the Rock on Which Our Republic Rests

God's Word makes the USA safe. That is why the biggest threat to our national security is the people not following the Bible.

Jesus said, *Whosoever... heareth my sayings, and doeth them, I will shew you to whom he is like: He is like a man which built an house, and digged deep, and laid the foundation on a rock: and when the flood arose, the stream beat vehemently upon that house, and could not shake it: for it was founded upon a rock. But he that heareth, and doeth not, is like a man that without a foundation built an house upon the earth; against which the stream did beat vehemently, and immediately it fell; and the ruin... was great.* (Luke 6:47-49 KJV).

Next, we will learn how the USA's true ruler gives us protection and liberty.

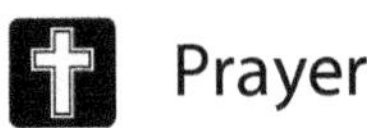

Father, Americans love Your Word. You are the USA's Lawgiver. We ask for the Holy Bible to fill our homes, government, schools, courts, and military. We agree that Christianity is part of the common law. In Jesus' name. Amen.

1. *What is Jesus Christ telling us in Luke 6:46-49?*
2. *Why does God protect us for having the Bible as the Rock on which our Republic rests? Give examples.*
3. *Is the LORD your lawgiver? Explain.*

6

Fourth Truth—Jesus Rules the USA

"The LORD is our King..."
Isaiah 33:22 KJV

Tensions were high. Resistance to tyrants was publicly viewed as obedience to God and liberty for every American. England saw that the people of our nation were confident that Jesus wanted them to obey Him, not King George. The English appointed governor of Boston reported in 1774, *If you ask an American, who is his master? He will tell you he has none, nor any governor but Jesus Christ.*[1]

Patriotically, our founders sounded, *No king but King Jesus,* as an American Revolution motto. This famous battle cry affirms that Jesus Christ rules our nation and the USA lives for Him. This is why we are *One Nation Under God!*

They recognized Jesus' authority and we need to follow their example and confess that Jesus is our King and authority.

Obeying Jesus Makes America Great

Every person has a king. Who is your king? The person that you obey is your ruler. There are two choices:

- Jesus Christ – the King of the Kingdom of God, or
- The devil – the king of the power of darkness.

Everyone serves one of these two kings, Jesus Christ or Satan. However, choosing the right king makes the difference between living in:

- Light, truth, protection and liberty with King Jesus, or
- Darkness, lies, danger and tyranny with the devil.

This is important because each of us will give an account of our lives to Jesus Christ on the Judgment Day, so we must follow Him (2 Corinthians 5:10). We are stewards of what God has given us and want to hear Christ say, "Well done," to our work (Matthew 25:21 KJV).

You must make the decision that Jesus is your King, since after Adam's fall people are naturally born under the sinful nature. The people not following Jesus Christ are under Satan's power, even if they serve themselves or a person in sin (Colossians 1:13).

Who we follow is an urgent matter that affects the safety of our daily lives and the future of the USA. We see our country's survival is at stake with many troubles—from politicians opposing our God-given rights to terrorism.

Fourth Bible Truth to make the USA great *Isaiah 33:22, Phil. 2:11*	**Have no king but King Jesus** *Why? Jesus brings the Kingdom of God's blessings, including protection and liberty.*

The Fourth Bible Truth is God protects you, gives you liberty, justice, and righteousness, and saves the USA for having "no king but King Jesus". America is great because of having Jesus as our King. Disobeying Jesus means there is danger, tyranny, injustice, and sin. But with King Jesus we are free from communism, globalists, and the New World Order.

In power and majesty Jesus reigns, whether we submit to Him or not. Psalm 47:7-9 says, *For God is the King of all the earth: sing ye praises with understanding. God reigneth over the heathen: God sitteth upon the throne of his holiness... the shields of the earth belong unto God: he is greatly exalted.*

Jesus Christ Is the Sovereign of the Universe

Since Jesus is the ruler of everything, we are to live exalting Him above every other person. God testifies, *That at the name of Jesus every knee should bow, of things in heaven, and things in earth, and things under the earth; And that every tongue should confess that Jesus Christ is Lord, to the glory of God the Father* (Philippians 2:10-11 KJV).

We honor Him as superior to all political leaders for He is the *KING OF KINGS, AND LORD OF LORDS* (Revelation 19:16; 1:5, 1 Tim. 6:15 KJV). He is subject to no one, but the Father, and all things are subject to Him. All things are done according to His counsel and all authority in heaven and earth has been given to Him (Colossians 1:16, Matthew 28:18).

Jesus sits at the right hand of God the Father. Higher than the angels, His throne is forever and ever; of His Kingdom there shall be no end (Hebrews 1:8, Luke 1:33). We know that His wrath is on the earthly leaders who don't follow Him (Psalm 2:2-5). Pharaoh found out the LORD is a man of war.

Jesus was in the beginning with God; He is our Creator. All things were made by Him with the Father and Holy Spirit (John 1:1-3). We exalt Him because He is God and in Him all things exist (Hebrews 1:2-3, 6, Colossians 1:17). The earth and the heavens will perish, but He will always exist (2 Peter 3:10-11). He is the Alpha and the Omega, the Beginning and the End, the First and the Last (Revelation 22:13).

As the Judge of mankind, we have confidence that He will not acquit the wicked. He knows everything about everyone and He knows more about each person than even they know of themselves. He pardons the sins of all who come to Him.

Along with the Father and the Holy Spirit, Jesus Christ is Elohim (our Creator), Jehovah (my LORD God), Adonai (master and Lord), El Shaddai (God Almighty, my supply, my nourishment), Jehovah Jireh (my provider), Jehovah Rapha (my healer), Jehovah Nissi (my banner, victory), Jehovah Mikadesh (my sanctifier), Jehovah Tsidkenu (my righteousness), Jehovah Shalom (my peace), Jehovah Rohi (my shepherd), and Jehovah Shammah (the LORD is there). Jesus Christ is the great I AM.

Having no king but King Jesus isn't reserved only for when we get to Heaven. It is a daily, moment-by-moment walk with Him that gives you God's favor instead of alienation. Think how much favor God gives you when you say Jesus is your King. To live with Jesus as your leader, first acknowledge Him as your King. Then during the day thank Him for His goodness and obey Him by faith, submitting to His authority (Matthew 16:24).

Why do we say, "Jesus Christ is Lord of the USA"? The answer is the USA has the Kingdom of God blessings through Him. We have liberty, prosperity, peace, brotherly love, and every good thing. To be free of dictators, Shariah law, and corruption, then daily live with Jesus Christ as the leader of our nation. Where He rules, there are no evil rulers. That is why tyrants oppose Christianity, but Jesus is stronger than all evil persons. He removes corruption to protect His people.

Is Jesus Your King?

Let's look at four common levels of having Jesus as our King. The following shows where people are at:

1. **Rebellion** – This person serves self or man not King Jesus.
2. **Mental assent that Jesus is King** – Many Christians are at this level where they agree that Jesus is their King but don't pray and think when making decision, "What does Jesus want me to do?"
3. **Partial surrender to the KING OF KINGS** – At this level, a person is willing to obey God but only occasionally takes a public stand for Jesus Christ.
4. **Total surrender to King Jesus** – This is the level God desires. We see the disciples left all and followed Jesus. Also, the founding fathers obeyed Jesus and proclaimed: "no king but King Jesus" instead of man. At this level, Jesus defeats your enemies continuously.

Our founders taught it is our duty to do God's will. So if Jesus is your leader, you "obey God rather than men" (Acts 5:29 KJV).

Americans have "No King but King Jesus"

Americans believe it is our country's duty to serve God and that human authority is under God's authority. That is one reason why real Americans have Jesus as their leader. Famous American pastors, like Jonas Clark, taught that "God is governor among the nations" from Psalm 22:28 (KJV).

The good news is it is easy for our nation to have abundant blessings again. The key is to realize all blessings come through Jesus Christ.

Another important place where President Donald Trump and Vide-President Mike Pence obey God is working to get rid of the corrupt Johnson Amendment that silences non-profit churches from speaking about politics. This is a priority to make the USA great, because it shows that Jesus is King, not tyranny. By removing the Johnson Amendment, we have God's favor. Every pastor and Christian should boldly speak up for God, even with the corrupt Johnson Amendment, which the Holy Bible and the First Amendment say is illegal.

To glorify God and so Americans have freedom, the Gospel of Jesus Christ must never be compromised. You may have realized that Churches that won't speak up politically can't save the USA. All glory to God; because I teach the Gospel I am seeing revival nationwide. The USA is a covenant Christian nation and it is our duty to keep and protect our nation that belongs to God for God's glory.

Our liberty-loving nation must have *no king but King Jesus,* so we are on God's side and have His freedom. Will you affirm that Jesus is the USA's King? If so, then with love for God in your heart, share with as many people as you can, *The LORD is our king; He will save us* (Isaiah 33:22 KJV).

Next, we discover an easy tool to share the good news and raise up the next generations as godly Americans.

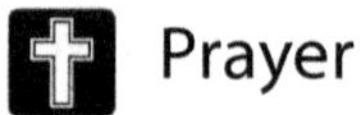

Prayer

Father, Jesus Christ is my King and the King of the USA. The USA obeys Him, not anyone else. We thank You that right now He is removing everything against Him from the USA. In Jesus' name. Amen.

✓ Reflection Questions

1. *How do you live with no king but King Jesus? Explain.*
2. *Why do those refusing to call Jesus King cause God's judgment on our nation?*
3. *Why did God greatly bless our founders and Moses for obeying Him rather than ungodly rule?*
4. *With more people calling on Jesus as King of the USA, what additional blessings would you have?*

7
Fifth Truth—Disciple Hearts to Be Like Jesus

"Teaching them to observe all things whatsoever I have commanded you..." Jesus
Matthew 28:20 KJV

God desires for our nation to have hearts like Jesus, so we glorify God and do good to man. Living like Jesus makes our citizens exceptional. Our forefathers faithfully advanced the Kingdom of God to help America grow in Christ, with piety and virtue. As stewards, they discipled the USA as their priority. Now it is our turn to teach to observe all things Jesus commanded us. We will have great wisdom and injustice will end (Matthew 28:19-20).

Jesus gave us the Great Commission and He said that part of our vital work for Him is *that repentance and remission of sins should be preached in His name among all nations* (Luke 24:47 KJV). The *all nations* includes our beloved USA.

The Fifth Bible Truth is God will protect you and prosper the USA by making disciples of the country. Keeping covenant to raise godly generations creates a safe nation with upright and law-abiding citizens instead of a country with crime and riots. Making Christian disciples of our nation makes the USA exceptional. But it is ignoble to have children who do not know God's Word and live in sin.

Fifth Bible Truth to make the USA great *Matt. 28:19-20, Is. 59:21*	**Make disciples of the USA** *Why? To raise godly generations.*

We should often ask ourselves, "What can we do for God and country?" We can teach that the LORD is the God of our nation and help put Bible reading back in every school. Let's make disciples. This is the next step to make the USA great.

12 American Ways to Make Disciples

To have hearts like Jesus, teach the following:

1. **Serve the LORD only**—not strange gods or anything else. *Matthew 4:10, Exodus 20:3*
2. **Have no king but King Jesus:** God is sovereign; we obey God's government. *Isaiah 9:6 & 33:22, Philippians 2:11, Revelation 19:6, 2 Timothy 2:12*
3. **Demand Christian religious liberty:** We advance the Kingdom of our Lord Jesus. *Mark 12:30, Gal. 5:1*
4. **Man is created with dignity:** Americans demand our God-given unalienable rights—*including life, liberty, the pursuit of happiness, property, and conscience. Genesis 1:27, Acts 5:29, Declaration of Independence*

5. **The USA has traditional marriage only**—One man and one woman; we believe in sexual purity with no adultery or fornication. *Jude 7, 1 Corinthians 6:9-11*
6. **Instruct children to know God:** Daily read the Holy Bible and have Christian prayer in schools. *Isaiah 59:21*
7. **The LORD is our Lawgiver:** God only blesses Christian laws based on the Bible. *Luke 6:47-49, Is. 33:22*
8. **Work to have a covenant Christian nation Government** immediately that:
   1) Are Christians who fear God Ex. 18:21, 2 Cor. 6:14-18
   2) Calls for Christian religious liberty Mark 12:30, Gal. 5:1
   3) Insists we have God-given rights Gen 1:27, Acts 5:29
   4) Is truthful Exodus 18:21
   5) Hates covetousness Exodus 18:21
9. **Support Christians** in politics, business, and organizations—not the heathen. *2 Chronicles 19:2*
10. **Our Christian nation is pro-life.** *Matthew 5:17*
11. **Serve God, not mammon (money).** *Matthew 6:24*
12. **Biblically pray for government**. Pray daily for the people of our nation and government to live the five points of #7 above. You can get a prayer brochure at www.USA.church.

In addition, you and your church are invited to participate in: (1) Nationwide prayer and fasting for our country on Wednesdays; (2) Christians Uniting to Save the USA™; and (3) The American Disciple Making Team™. See www.USA.church for more information.

Next, we discover how to have victory over sin.

Father, the USA serves You. Help us make disciples of our nation. In Jesus' name. Amen.

1. *Why must the USA be discipled?*
2. *History affirms that raising godly generations makes America wealthy. Why is this?*
3. *Our founders had the government disciple the nation with Christianity practiced in schools, printing the Holy Bible, and evangelism outreaches. What can you do to help these great works return to government?*
4. *In what ways can you help teach these 12 American ways to follow Jesus? What can your church do?*

8

Sixth Truth—Victory Over Sin

"He took courage,
and put away the abominable idols..."
2 Chronicles 15:8 KJV

History is filled with holy conflict when God's people rise up and publicly turn from their wicked ways and sinful relationships. With great courage King Asa and the people arose to stop the apathy about sin, so their troubles from God's judgment would end. As they used to do in Old Testament times before Jesus Christ came, the Bible shows that Judah killed the wicked people (2 Chronicles 15).

King Josiah also loved God and did the same (2 Kings 23:4-24). Likewise, in holy conflict Moses boldly called those on the LORD's side to kill the people refusing to repent, so God wouldn't destroy Israel when the people forsook Him by turning away from God to worship a molten calf (Exodus 32).

Today we remove evil differently; we *turn away* from those who refuse to repent (2 Timothy 3:5, Romans 16:7, 1

Corinthians 5:13, James 4:7). God wants us free of evil so we simply *separate* ourselves from those against God. We read the Old Testament accounts of killing through the New Testament lens to identify and *turn away* from those in rebellion to God.

The Sixth Bible Truth is turning away from everything against Jesus Christ protects us, prevents an economic collapse and secures our financial future, defends Christianity, and helps a greater number of people go to heaven instead of hell.

The people serving Jesus make the USA great, since they no longer do the devil's will. God says those who refuse to repent of their sins endanger the nation with the curse of *thou shalt not prosper in thy ways* (Deuteronomy 28:29 KJV). On the other hand, the Holy Bible shows that repenting ends economic troubles (2 Chronicles 7:13-14, Matthew 6:33).

To make the USA great, the Christian church, as the true leader of the nation under God, must unite and repent of sins. Not doing so means we live in darkness and lies, under Satan's power. Not repenting can result in an invasion or removal of the USA, as happened to Israel.

Sixth Bible Truth to make the USA great *2 Tim. 3:5, 2 Chron. 15:8*	**Turn away from everything against Jesus Christ** *Why? To love God and to heal our land.*

Every day we are to remember that God is holy. To have safety and God's favor, we must turn away from sin. To live in victory over sin the Bible says, *Submit yourselves therefore to God. Resist the devil, and he will flee from you.* (James 4:7 KJV).

If you agree with God for the USA to repent of sin, you are an American hero. Here are five major sins to repent of that cause God's judgment.

1. False gods - Other gods provoke the LORD to wrath, since forsaking Him is a covenant breaking act. As Christians, we know the Bible forbids turning to false religions and cults, such as Buddhists, Hindus, Muslims, Jehovah's Witnesses, Scientologists, and Mormons. Serving money instead of God is also a false god.

- "Thou shalt worship the Lord thy God, and him only shalt thou serve." (Matthew 4:10 KJV)
- See Galatians 1:9, Matthew 6:24

Let's look at when Aaron the high priest and the Israelites made their own god, a molten calf, to go before them instead of the LORD. The people saw Moses was delayed in returning with God's instructions. Some thought Moses died, but he was seeking God for Israel's future (Exodus 32).

By not trusting in God and seeking deliverance another way, the people committed spiritual adultery to God. Aaron didn't stop the people from going astray with false gods, but misled them and fashioned a molten calf and said, *These be thy gods, O Israel, which brought thee up out of the land of Egypt* (Exodus 32:4 KJV). Then they celebrated their man-made god and caused shame with immorality and called this a feast unto the LORD.

They were breaking covenant, which provoked God. But Moses asked God to turn from His fierce wrath. Then Moses confronted Aaron and burned the molten calf in fire and ground it to powder; he scattered it on the water and made the Israelites drink it. God and Moses responded this way because other gods are God's enemies leading into darkness.

Moses told them they *sinned a great sin* (Exodus 32:30 KJV). To spare the people and families that would repent from the judgment for this sin, Moses made everyone make a decision, asking, *Who is on the LORD's side? let him come unto Me* (Exodus 32:26 KJV). God's response was to kill those who wouldn't follow Him and plague the people for their god. This serious response is because they forsook God.

From this example, we learn how God views His people turning to the world for help. We see that Moses didn't sin but did what God said and killed about 3,000 rebellious men. Some say this is harsh, but forsaking God meant everyone would have been destroyed and not enter the promised land. Recall, today we don't kill those against God, but what we do is "turn away" from those who won't follow God.

Paul warned us not to receive those who preach another Jesus or another spirit or another gospel (2 Corinthians 11:4). He also taught, *If any man preach any other gospel unto you than that ye have received, let him be accursed* (Galatians 1:9 KJV). Should you vote for someone like that? If God says they are accursed, why would you want them in the White House or on a school board?

We know God says, *Adulterers and adulteresses... friendship of the world is enmity with God... whosoever therefore will be a friend of the world is the enemy of God* (James 4:4 KJV).

This is a good time to ask God's forgiveness for turning to Mormons for help instead of God's people. Millions of people, including many popular ministers, have disobeyed God and turned to Mormons Glenn Beck and Mitt Romney.

Mormons do not have God's answers and turning to them politically bring God's wrath (Ezekiel 23). This is a great sin similar to Aaron making the molten calf and making a feast to the LORD that caused many to die and plagued the people (Exodus 32). Some may think it doesn't matter who they voted for in 2012, but this and other times people voted for non-Christians must be confessed to restore God's protection.

To be forgiven by God, pray: *Father, You are the one true God. We ask You to forgive the USA for turning to Mormons and other false ways in politics and elsewhere. We trust in You. In Jesus' name. Amen.*

As a note, for President Trump to be one of the greatest presidents ever, the Bible teaches he must say, "The Lord is the one true God. All other gods are false. Also, God commands marriage to be a man and a woman."

2. Homosexual sin - God is for the marriage of one man and one woman for a lifetime, and doing this brings us God's safety. The truth is Jesus Christ makes families strong. That means we are to turn from sexual sins, including fornication, adultery, and sodomy. The Bible says:

- "Be not deceived: neither fornicators... nor adulterers, nor effeminate, nor abusers of themselves with mankind... shall inherit the kingdom of God" (1 Corinthians 6:9-10 KJV).

Since God will destroy the USA if people rebel against Him with same-sex marriage, we must look at this further. God says:

- "The men of Sodom were wicked and sinners before the LORD exceedingly" (Genesis 13:13 KJV).
- "God gave them up unto vile affections: for even their women did change the natural use into that which is against nature: And likewise also the men, leaving the natural use of the woman, burned in their lust one toward another; men with men..." (Romans 1:26-27 KJV).
- God "turning the cities of Sodom and Gomorrha into ashes condemned them with an overthrow, making them an ensample unto those that after should live ungodly" (2 Peter 2:6 KJV).
- See Romans 1:24-32, Leviticus 18:22 & 25, and Jude 7

Our national security is very important. God says, *When the host goeth forth against thine enemies, then keep thee from every wicked thing (Deuteronomy 23:9 KJV)*. With sodomy and other sins in the military, God doesn't go with them. That puts our nation at stake. Will you let God know you are on His side and oppose sin?

Everyone loves and everyone hates. Do you love God and hate sin? Or do you love sin and hate God?

The LORD is our Lawgiver and Judge, so we must follow Him. Same-sex marriage is much more than sexual sin; it is defying God who created male and female.

Jesus said, *He that hath my commandments, and keepeth them, he it is that loveth me* (John 14:21KJV). Those who follow God are *lovers of God* (2 Timothy 3:4 KJV). Yet, sodomites call Christians, including our founders, "haters" and "bigots" for loving God. However, the Word of God calls homosexuals and other sinners "haters of God," since they oppose Him (Romans 1:30 KJV).

The truth is everyone loves and everyone hates. We either love God and hate sin, or we love sin and hate God. Light and darkness can not coexist. What kind of lover are you? Do you love God or sin? What type of hater are you? Do you hate sin or God? If you want to go to heaven, then love God. He says, *That they all might be damned who believed not the truth, but had pleasure in unrighteousness* (2 Thessalonians 2:12 KJV).

The Bible says the ungodly are at war with God. Jesus Christ explains why, *For every one that doeth evil hateth the light* (John 3:20 KJV). Liberals, who hate God, discriminated against and fired the CEO of Mozilla for supporting traditional marriage. That is why "hate crime laws" are corrupt. "Hate crime laws" were invented to bully everyone who follows God.

In his popular dictionary, Noah Webster defined sodomy using Romans 1 as "A crime against nature." For God to bless the military, Washington, the most respected American, court martialed sodomites and had, "Abhorrence and Detestation of such Infamous Crimes."[1] Since "hate crime laws" would put in jail God and the founding fathers, it is obvious these "laws" are unBiblical and unAmerican. The USA either does God's will like our founders say to do with laws against sin and God blesses our lives, or the nation opposes God and is cursed.

Scientifically, research show greater health issues with sodomites. The CDC reports that two in five homosexuals have HIV and get 57% of the new HIV cases,[2] and studies show their average age of death is between 39 - 43 years old.[3]

What is the most Christ-like and compassionate response to sodomites and other sinners? Jesus shows us. He said, *Repent ye, and believe the Gospel* (Mark 1:15 KJV). He loves people and wants each of us to go to heaven instead of hell.

If the shamefulness of sodomy doesn't bother a person, it is a sign of becoming "a reprobate" (Romans 1:28 KJV), unapproved by God. Right away, that person must confess the sin, receive forgiveness by Jesus' blood, and cry out to God to fill them with the Holy Spirit, so they don't lose their soul.

God and the Constitution: Same-sex Marriage is Not law

Above all, the USA must obey the Word of God, which commands, *Thou shalt not lie with mankind, as with womankind: it is abomination (Leviticus 18:22 KJV).* God tells us same-sex marriage is not law. Then we follow the Constitution. Our founders wrote it and know what is constitutional. To do God's will they made homosexual sin illegal in all 13 colonies, as did all 50 states.

Pastors asking people to repent makes the USA great again.

Exercising our God-given right to freedom of Christian speech is guaranteed by the Bible and the Bill of Rights. We need every pastor to stand up for God's law, and then the law of the land, and say same-sex marriage is disobeying God and the Constitution.

Like our founding fathers, Mike Huckabee boldly defined it as "judicial tyranny" to jail Kim Davis because a high school civics class knows the Supreme Court can't make a law. Remember, the Constitution dictates that laws are made by congress and executed by the president.[4] Moreover, congress can't make a law against God, because the First Amendment says, *Congress shall make no law... prohibiting the free exercise [of Christianity].* We are to always remember that laws against Christians are illegal!

Just think how many people end up in hell by homosexual marriage, including young people learning sinful ways in schools. After all, no one can change God's ordinance of marriage (James 4:4, Romans 1:24-32, Isaiah 24:5).

To stop God from destroying the USA for defying Him, we must pray and work for Christian leaders to replace those who hate God. He shows us how to respond to same-sex marriage. To establish law and order and restore God's protection, we and our churches are to:

- Cry out to Him to deliver us from the tyranny (Judges 3:9, 2 Corinthians 6:14-18).
- Boldly say the USA obeys God rather than men.
- Teach it is illegal to make a law against Christianity.

Remember, lives are at stake. To defend Christianity, pastors must preach to repent of sin. When was the last time your pastor taught to repent of these major sins? As it was in 1776, it is today. Bold pastors and Christians who insist that our nation serves Jesus Christ bring God's favor to us.

In summary, reasons to do God's will on marriage are:

- **To love God** - Our duty is to obey God's will of one man and one woman marriage (Matthew 19:4-6).
- **To go to Heaven** - God saved Lot who was vexed by the sin of the sodomites. But Lot's wife didn't fear God and lost her soul to hell where the worm shall not die and the fire is not quenched (2 Peter 2:6-9).

- **To save the USA** - God is to be feared. He promises that same-sex marriage means certain destruction of the country (Jude 7, 2 Peter 2:6, Leviticus 18:25).

3. Abortion - God is pro-life. That is why the USA is pro-life. He promises to heal our land by our nation repenting from shedding innocent blood. In its most base form, abortion is simply murder.

- "You shall not kill" (Matthew 5:21)
- "They sacrificed their sons and their daughters unto devils, and shed innocent blood" (Psalm 106:37 KJV).

When politicians promote sacrificing our children by spending about $1.5 billion in three years to abortion related companies, they break covenant and use our money against our consciences.[5] Our Christian duty is to never have government funded abortion and to bring back the ban on abortions to make the USA great again This will stop more innocent blood crying out to God, which results in leaders who hate Americans as God's judgment. This sin is a curse that is causing so many of the USA's problems (Psalm 106:37-42).

Here is hope. If you had an abortion or if you have guilt from another sin, ask God to cleanse your conscience with Jesus Christ's blood. God will remove the guilt (Hebrews 9:14). Jesus' blood will make you whole.

4. The Occult - Many are unaware of the dangers of Satan's darkness, but the devil uses movies, books, schools, social media, and other sources to influence people with familiar spirits, psychics, talking to the dead, sorcery, numerology, fortune telling, horoscopes, meditation with demons, and witches.

- "There shall not be found among you any one that maketh his son or his daughter to pass through the fire, or that useth divination, or an observer of times, or an enchanter, or a witch, or a charmer, or a consulter with familiar spirits, or a wizard, or a necromancer. For all that do these things are an abomination unto the LORD" (Deuteronomy 18:10-12 KJV).

5. The Lie of Separation of Church and State - There is an important message that pastors and Christians must teach and take action on to make the USA exceptional. We must declare our country follows the LORD and work for a government like our founders that gladly submits to the authority of God. Separation of church and state is:

1. Not what our founders or the USA practiced
2. Not Constitutional
3. Not historical
4. Sin that endangers the country's survival

The Word of God shows that government is to submit to God and recognize His sovereignty:

- "For the LORD is our judge, the LORD is our lawgiver, the LORD is our king" (Isaiah 33:22 KJV)
- "The government shall be upon his shoulder" (Isaiah 9:6 KJV)
- "Be wise now therefore, O ye kings: be instructed, ye judges of the earth. Serve the LORD with fear, and rejoice with trembling. Kiss the Son, lest he be angry, and ye perish from the way, when his wrath is kindled but a little. Blessed are all they that put their trust in him." (Psalm 2:10-12 KJV)

The good news is that times of refreshing come by repenting of everything against Jesus Christ.

Next, we will learn the hope of God's total forgiveness.

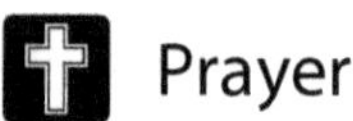

Father, I and the USA are on Your side. We repent of everything against Jesus Christ, including tolerance of other gods, turning to the heathen, abortion, homosexuality, the occult, and the lie of separation of church and state. In Jesus' name. Amen.

✓ Reflection Questions

1. *God calls us to repent of all sin. What are the major sins in this chapter that greatly endanger our nation's safety?*
2. *Explain why turning from sin makes the USA great?*
3. *What will you and your church do to help others repent and have victory over sin?*

9

Seventh Truth—God's Mercy and Forgiveness

"You are a gracious God, and merciful,
slow to anger, and of great kindness."
Jonah 4:2 KJV

It is not too late for the USA to receive God's mercy and forgiveness for our national sins. Why does God want to show mercy to the USA? He knows we need mercy for our great sins so our nation is not destroyed. False gods, same-sex marriage, and selling innocent aborted babies' body parts grieve the Holy Spirit. But God's mercy is greater than our sins.

We must confess our sins to God and be forgiven. This gives us hope and a new beginning.

To the woman caught in adultery Jesus said, *Neither do I condemn thee: go, and sin no more* (John 8:11 KJV). No one deserves forgiveness. We cannot earn it, or buy it. Yet, by putting our faith in Jesus for forgiveness we are forgiven.

God is Satisfied with the Sacrifice of Jesus

As the Lamb of God, Jesus laid down His life for us to redeem us from our sins, the innocent for the guilty. *For he hath made him to be sin for us, who knew no sin; that we might be made the righteousness of God in him.* (2 Cor. 5:21 KJV).

Seventh Bible Truth to make the USA great *1 John 1:7, Jonah 4:2*	**Restore the Cross and pray to receive forgiveness for the USA's sins by the sacrifice of Jesus** *Why? To restore God's favor and to live in grace.*

The curses from sin are removed by: (1) Atonement for our personal and national sins by Jesus Christ on the cross; and (2) Asking God to be forgiven. So the next Bible Truth has two parts: the cross brings back God's favor (atonement) and when we ask for forgiveness, then we live in God's grace.

The Seventh Bible Truth is restoring the cross and praying to receive forgiveness for the USA's sins by the sacrifice of Jesus will restore God's favor and grace to our lives and nation. Each of us and the USA are on the LORD's side when we believe that Jesus Christ's death on the cross forgives our sins.

Without Jesus there is no way to have God's favor. We are going to be forgiven and remove God's judgment now. Perhaps, the reason that Judah was destroyed after Josiah is because there was no atonement for Manasseh's sins. That is why we need to cleanse the USA from the sins of Obama and others. We don't want to share in their curse.

Restoring the altar of the LORD is part of what King Asa did to end judgment (2 Chronicles 15:8). When God plagued

Israel during King David's time, David built an altar to God and prayed and the plague ended (2 Samuel 24:25).

God remembers our covenant through Jesus who took God's wrath for our sins on the cross. Jesus is the altar, priest, and victim. That is why we put our faith in our Lord dying on the cross for us to restore the altar today. Restoring the Cross brings Heaven on earth—for you personally and for the USA.

Remember, Calvary's tree is God's answer to the analogy of the bricks falling and the sycamore tree being cut down in *The Harbinger* book. These *7 Bible Truths* give us the answer.

When Jesus forgave our sins on the cross, He was sealing and keeping covenant. His blood is the blood of the covenant. *the blood of Jesus Christ his Son cleanseth us from all sin.* (1 John 1:7 KJV). *He... put away sin by the sacrifice of Himself* (Hebrews 9:26 KJV).

The church receives forgiveness for the USA.

The blood of Jesus is more powerful than any sin. The nail prints Jesus has from the three nails when they crucified Him proves He loves us and paid the price for our sins. To be forgiven of your sins, pray: *Father, I confess my sins of ___. I am cleansed by Jesus Christ's blood. In Jesus' name. Amen.*

Pray and Receive Forgiveness for the USA

Do you feel sorrowful for our nation's sins. Our consciences are to convict us that it is shameful for boys to enter girls dressing rooms at schools and for teachers to have students read about the occult. The sins of our land stand out.

God expects us to weep and wail over them (James 4:9). They will either be forgiven by Jesus, or the USA will be punished.

The restoration of God's favor, by the cross and the blood of Jesus symbolized, ended the plague that killed 14,700 people because of the rebellion of Korah (Numbers 16:46-50).

Acknowledging the cross as a nation and humbling ourselves in covenant prayer to receive forgiveness for the country's sins make the USA great. On the other hand, ignoring Jesus' death and refusing to ask for forgiveness results in a curse and greatly endangers the nation.

To restore jobs, have liberty, get out of debt, remove terrorism, and protect our environment, we must ask for forgiveness (1 John 1:9, 2 Chronicles 7:14). Let's approach God in prayer with holy reverence.

Next, we will fully restore God's blessings.

 Prayer to Forgive the USA's Sins

Father,

You are merciful. The USA restores the cross. With godly sorrow Americans ask for Your mercy for our sins instead of Your judgment. John 8:11, Jonah 4:2, Amos 5:18

The USA confesses and repents of:

- *Other gods* Matthew 4:10
- *Homosexuality, adultery and fornication* Jude 7, 1 Corinthians 6:9-10
- *Not having Christian religious liberty as our priority as a nation* Mark 12:30

- *The places we don't follow Jesus in government, schools, courts and the military, and taking the Holy Bible & Christian prayer out of schools* 2 Timothy 2:12, Isaiah 59:21
- *Not demanding our God-given rights of life, liberty, the pursuit of happiness, property, and conscience* Genesis 1:27, Acts 5:29
- *Helping the wicked instead of supporting Christians in politics and business* 2 Timothy 3:5, 2 Chronicles 19:2, 2 Corinthians 6:14-18
- *Abortion* Matthew 5:17
- *Unjust wars* Mark 12:31
- *Coveting* Matthew 6:24, Ephesians 5:5
- *Occult, sorcery, and witchcraft* Deuteronomy 18:10-12
- *All other sins* 2 Chronicles 7:14

We receive forgiveness for our personal and national sins by the sacrifice of Jesus. 1 John 1:7 & 9

In Jesus' name. Amen.

1. *What is the meaning of 1 John 1:7?*
2. *Are you confident your sins are forgiven? Why?*
3. *Why does asking God to forgive the USA give you safety and improve the economy?*

10

Covenant Protection and Abundance

"Blessed is the nation whose God is the LORD..."
Psalm 33:12 KJV

We have learned that God wants us to give Him our hearts re-affirming: The LORD is the God of the USA and Americans are His people. Insisting to have Christian religious liberty with our *One Nation Under God* covenant relationship is what makes America great.

By learning the *7 Bible Truths*, we can now fully live them out. We are going to seal our covenant, so prepare your heart before God because this is holy. As Jesus Christ purchased our salvation with His blood, He purchased the USA to be His covenant Christian nation. Because God gives Americans everything in covenant, will you let Him know that you submit yourself and the USA entirely to Him?

Kings Asa and Josiah rejoiced to covenant with God when they recognized Judah was in danger for their sin.

7 BIBLE TRUTHS MAKE THE USA GREAT

First Bible Truth *Psalm 33:12, 2 Cor. 6:18*	**Re-affirm Covenant: The LORD is the God of the USA and Americans are His people** *Why? To get the USA in right relationship with God.*
Second Bible Truth *2 Chron. 15:12, Matt. 7:7*	**Seek God with all your heart and all your soul** *Why? To find and His Help.*
Third Bible Truth *Luke 6:47-49, 2 Chron. 34:31*	**Obey the Holy Bible with all your heart and all your soul** *Why? To do God's will.*
Fourth Bible Truth *Isaiah 33:22, Phil. 2:11*	**Have no king but King Jesus** *Why? Jesus brings the Kingdom of God's blessings, including protection and liberty.*
Fifth Bible Truth *Matt. 28:19-20, Is. 59:21*	**Make disciples of the USA** *Why? To raise godly generations.*
Sixth Bible Truth *2 Tim. 3:5, 2 Chron. 15:8*	**Turn away from everything against Jesus Christ** *Why? To love God.*
Seventh Bible Truth *1 John 1:7, Jonah 4:2*	**Restore the Cross and receive forgiveness for the USA's sins by the sacrifice of Jesus** *Why? To restore God's favor and to live in grace.*

The *7 Bible Truths* are the American breakthrough secret that always works. The only way to protect the next generations is for them to walk with Jesus Christ. Covenant gives us confidence to have Americanism, not globalism.

Unfortunately, we were taught to be politically correct and that false religions were to be present in our schools, military, and government. Then those outside of covenant tried to take our Christian faith away which led to the great judgments and even the danger of a final judgment. But we hold fast and say no! The LORD is the God of the USA!

Will You Join Covenant?

The Jamestown Settlers, Pilgrims, and others show us how a few people by faith can turn a heathen land to be the strongest Christian nation ever. Now, we must work to make the USA the greatest Christian nation ever. Here are questions to ask yourself to see if you love God and country:

7 Questions to Seal the USA's Covenant with God

1. Do I publicly say: The LORD is the God of the USA and Americans are His people?
2. Am I seeking God with all my heart and all my soul, including for our nation?
3. Do I speak up for the USA to obey the Holy Bible?
4. Am I living with Jesus as King of the USA?
5. Will I help make disciples of our nation?
6. Do I speak up for our nation to turn away from everything against Jesus Christ?
7. Have I restored the cross and prayed to receive forgiveness for the USA's sins by Jesus' blood?

If you answer yes to these questions, you are on the LORD's side and He invites you to join covenant. You must agree to be in covenant. As you get ready to pray, thank the LORD that He is our God. Then examine yourself if there is any sin you can confess to God. By sealing covenant the devil's works are destroyed (1 John 3:8). Like our founders, we join God and country together forever. Americans love God!

To re-affirm covenant, pray and sign the following prayer. As an individual, family, or church, you may want to take communion as this is a holy covenant through Jesus Christ.

MAKE THE USA GREAT

Pray and Live: The USA's Covenant with God

Father,

You are holy. We thank You that the USA is dedicated to You in covenant to all generations.

LORD, You are the God of the USA and Americans are Your people. We seek You and obey the Holy Bible with all our hearts and all our souls. Jesus is our King, so our nation makes Christian disciples and we turn away from everything against Jesus Christ.

To do Your will, the USA agrees with You that marriage is one man and one woman only, the Bible is to be read in schools with Christian prayer, and abortion is to be banned again. We work and pray for covenant Christian leaders to immediately replace those disobeying You.

We thank You for the Cross and by Jesus' blood we receive forgiveness for the USA's sins.

In Jesus' name. Amen.

____

Your Name

We make the USA secure and strong when we let God know that we agree with Him and not the Supreme Court's rebellious, anti-God opinions, including same-sex marriage, removing our founder's Christianity from schools, abortion, and separation of church and state. These covenant breaking acts, along with false gods and voting for unbelievers, endanger our loved ones and nation with God's judgment.

You can print and put *The USA's Covenant with God* on your refrigerator, by your desk, and inside your church or ministry's bulletins to re-affirm it often. You can also take a picture of it to save and share it. On the second Sunday of each month, join our nation in praying our covenant to make the USA great. At my website, www.USA.church, there are free resources to use in your home, church, work, and school.

Now, let's live the real American Dream *to advance the Kingdom of our Lord Jesus Christ and to enjoy the liberties of the Gospel in purity and peace.*[1] While we have work to do to be exceptional throughout the nation in our families, education, business, and churches, we know re-affirming and daily living this covenant gives us God's protection and prosperity. Together, let's do all we can for God and country. By following Jesus, the USA is great!

☑ Reflection Questions

1. *How does covenant with God give you hope?*
2. *Why does Jesus make the USA great?*
3. *Who can you and your church invite to join covenant?*

Thank you for reading this inspirational book to bring God's protection, strength, and prosperity to your life and the nation. The next steps to help make the USA great are to seek God how you can share:

- JESUS MAKES AMERICA GREAT™
- **The 7 Bible Truths**

I invite you and your church to join:

- **One Million Americans on the LORD's Side**™
- The American Disciple Making Team™
- The Daily Biblical Prayer for Government™
- Wednesdays: Nationwide Prayer and Fasting™
- Christians Uniting to Save the USA™

REFERENCES

1 Who Makes America Great?

[1] "The USA is a Christian Republic," usa.church, January 26, 2016, https://www.usa.church/usa-christian-republic/

[2] George Washington, Presidential Proclamation, (October 3, 1789)

[4] " Trump: Unshackle Churches From Johnson Amendment," dailywire.com, October 3, 2016, http://www.dailywire.com/news/9649/trump-unshackle-churches-johnson-amendment-robert-kraychik#

[5] "Men Flood Target to Film Teen Girls after Allowing Males in Female Changing Rooms," freedomoutpost.com, June 18, 2016, http://freedomoutpost.com/men-flood-target-to-film-teen-girls-after-allowing-males-in-female-changing-rooms/

[6] "THE TRUTH ABOUT THE NEW YORK BOMBING," infowars.com, September 18, 2016, http://www.infowars.com/the-truth-about-the-new-york-bombing/

[7] "Donald J. Trump Statement on Preventing Muslim Immigration," usa.church, December 7, 2015, https://www.donaldjtrump.com/press-releases/donald-j.-trump-statement-on-preventing-muslim-immigration

[8] "Traditional-marriage 'hero' Roy Moore removed from office," wnd.com, September 30, 2016, http://www.wnd.com/2016/09/traditional-marriage-hero-roy-moore-removed-from-office

[9] "Mike Huckabee: We Must Stand with Kim Davis Against 'Criminalization of Christianity', breitbart.com, September 7, 2015, http://bit.ly/1Lfftkm

[10] "Noah Webster," webstersdictionary1828.com, Accessed January 24, 2015, http://webstersdictionary1828.com/NoahWebster

[11] "American Minute for September 13," americanminute.com, Accessed January 26, 2017, http://www.americanminute.com/index.php?date=09-13

2 First Truth: Covenant with the One True God

[1] Dr. Paul Jehle, Plymouth Rock Foundation, "July 2012 E News," *plymrock.org,* July, 2012, http://www.plymrock.org/july2012news.php

[2] The Pilgrims, Mayflower Compact, (November 11, 1620)

[3] John Winthrop, A Model of Christian Charity, (1630)

[4] Yale Law School, "The Articles of Confederation of the United Colonies of New England; May 19, 1643," *avalon.law.yale.edu,* accessed January 12, 2015, http://avalon.law.yale.edu/17th_century/art1613.asp

[5] John C. Fitzpatrick, The Writings of George Washington from the Original Manuscript Sources 1745-1799 Volume 15 May 6, 1779-July 28, 1779, (Library of Congress, 1939), 55

[6] Supreme Court, Church of the Holy Trinity v. United States, (Feb. 29, 1892)

[7] Gallup CEO Jim Clifton Interview on Fox News, *youtube.com,* February 5, 2015, https://www.youtube.com/watch?v=CTRAibMiLZ8

[8] "It's official: America is now No. 2," *marketwatch.com,* December 4, 2014, http://www.marketwatch.com/story/its-official-america-is-now-no-2-2014-12-04, and

"Does size matter? China poised to overtake US as world's largest economy in 2014," *ft.com,* April 30, 2014, http://blogs.ft.com/the-world/2014/04/does-size-matter-china-poised-to-overtake-us-as-worlds-largest-economy-in-2014/

[9] John Whiting and Henry Whiting, Revolutionary Orders of General Washington: Issued During the Years 1778, '80, '81, & '82 (New York and London, Wiley and Putnam, 1844) 32

[10] John Hancock, Massachusetts Governor's Proclamation, (October 15, 1791)

3 American Secrets for Safe and Blessed Lives

[1] Sir William Blackstone, Commentaries on the Laws of England: In Four Books... Volume 1, (New York, W. E. Dean, 1838), 94

[2] Sir William Blackstone, Commentaries on the Laws of England: In the Order, and Compiled from... (London, Saunders and Benning, 1840), 20

[3] The Law Journal for 1806; Consisting of Original Communications..., (London, W. Clarke and Sons, 1807), 106

[4] Joseph Story, Commentaries on the Constitution of the United States: With a ..., Volume 3, (Boston, Hilliard, Gray, and Company, 1833), 728

[5] Noah Webster, History of the United States, (New-Haven..., 1832), 299-300

5 Third Truth: Living the Bible Way

[1] Sir William Blackstone, Commentaries on the Laws of England: In Four Books..., (Philadelphia, J.B. Lippincott & Co., 1859), Page 28

[2] W. C. Anderson, Review of Dr. Scott's Bible and Politics in the Light of Religion and the Law, (San Francisco, Towne and Bacon, 1858), 75

[3] James Wilson, The Works of the Honourable James Wilson... Vol. 1, (Philadelphia, Lorenzo Press,1804), 104-105

6 Fourth Truth: Jesus Rules the Nation

[1] Elizabeth Cooper, Popular History of America..., (London: Longman, Green, Longman, Roberts, & Green, 1865), 399

8 Sixth Truth: Victory Over Sin

[1] John Whiting and Henry Whiting, Revolutionary Orders of General Washington: Issued During the Years 1778, '80, '81, & '82 (New York and London, Wiley and Putnam, 1844) 32

[2] "Prevalence and Awareness of HIV Infection Among Men Who Have Sex With Men..." cdc.gov, September 24, 2010, http://www.cdc.gov/mmwr/preview/mmwrhtml/mm5937a2.htm

[3] "New Study Shows Homosexuals Live 20 Fewer Years," *freerepublic.com,* June 6, 2005, http://www.freerepublic.com/focus/news/1417935/posts

[4] "Mike Huckabee blasts same-sex marriage ruling," foxnews.com, June 29, 2015, http://www.foxnews.com/transcript/2015/06/29/mike-huckabee-blasts-same-sex-marriage-ruling

[5] "GAO Confirms... Abortion Advocates Spent About $1.5 Billion in Tax Dollars," *cnsnews.com,* March 26, 2015, http://bit.ly/1ODgTdg

10 First Truth Reprise: Covenant Blessings and Favor

[1] Yale Law School, "The Articles of Confederation of the United Colonies of New England; May 19, 1643," *avalon.law.yale.edu,* accessed January 12, 2015, http://avalon.law.yale.edu/17th_century/art1613.asp

Prayer of Salvation

To become a Christian, pray a prayer like this:

Father,

I thank You that Jesus Christ died on the cross to forgive my sins. I confess with my mouth the Lord Jesus and I believe in my heart that You raised Jesus from the dead. I ask You for the Holy Spirit.

In Jesus' name. Amen. (John 3:16, Romans 10:9-10)

To grow as a Christian, pray and read the Holy Bible daily. I recommend reading a chapter or more in the morning and a chapter or more before sleeping. Then think about Bible verses during the day.

Across the nation, people ask me what Bible version I use. I love the King James Version (KJV).

If you prayed to be a Christian, let me know at USA Christian Church. The website is:

www.USA.church

Books by Steven Andrew

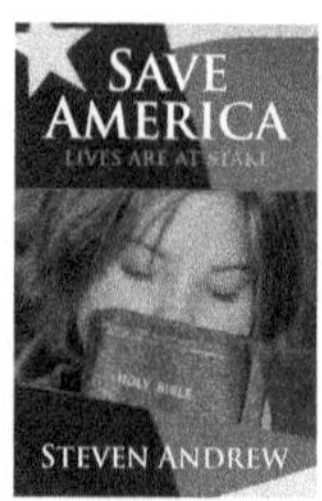

Save America

Paperback: ISBN 9780977955084
eBook: ISBN 9780977955046

"Save America," an expanded version of "Jesus Makes America Great," focuses on having God's protection for our lives and loved ones.

Love God and Love One Another

Paperback: ISBN 9780977955039
eBook: ISBN 9780977955084

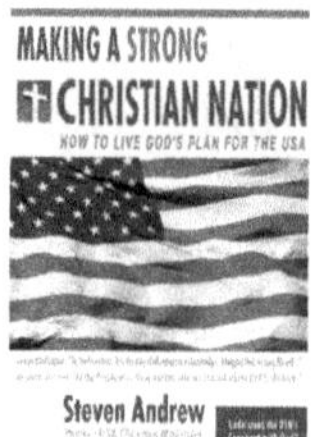

Making A Strong Christian Nation

Paperback: ISBN 9780977955077

Check for these upcoming new books:

The American Disciple Making Team™ Handbook

Are You an American?

One Million Americans on the LORD's Side

If you believe **JESUS MAKES AMERICA GREAT**, I invite you to join *One Million Americans on the LORD's Side* at www.USA.church.

One Million Americans

On the LORD's Side

Saving the USA

"Blessed is the nation whose God is the LORD" Psalm 33:12

Become a Partner, T-shirts, Coffee Mugs, and Items to Help Share the Gospel

To become a monthly partner or to give a one-time gift to USA Christian Church to help make the USA exceptional, and for a full list of apparel and other products, see www.USA.church. The proceeds go to sharing the Gospel.

www.ingramcontent.com/pod-product-compliance
Lightning Source LLC
Chambersburg PA
CBHW071833020426
42331CB00007B/1708

* 9 7 8 0 9 9 8 6 6 8 2 9 1 *